Written by: Despina Mavridou

Text editing: Christina Skroumpelou

Translation in English: Chrysoula Verikiou

Illustration: Korina Marnelaki

Country: Greece

1st edition December 2020

Contact details

Despina Mavridou

despoina.mavridou@gmail.com

Facebook page: https://www.facebook.com/Mum-dad-can-you-hear-me-103219515043344

"The higher the two Egos rose,
the deeper they drowned
their most magnificent creation,
their own child"

"Wednesday, November 18th 2019,

My dearest diary,

Something really weird happened yesterday. I was sleeping deeply and dreaming about my cancelled Math test, when a noise suddenly woke me up and got me out of bed. I was trying to figure out what all that noise was - until I recognized my Dad's voice. Mum and Dad were arguing again.

I tried to eavesdrop, although Grandma says we shouldn't do that.

I guess she's right. I'm a young lady now. I'm gonna be ten soon.

Mum was telling Dad to leave home and go to his girlfriend's house. I couldn't understand who that "girlfriend" was - and why Mum didn't like her . One thing was for sure, that girlfriend of his – really made my Mum angry. After a while, I must have gone back to sleep as I can't remember what happened next. At breakfast, though, we all kept silent, except Dad told me they wanted to talk to me in the evening. I can't figure out what they want to tell me. I asked my Teddy Bear, but he doesn't know either. I'm so anxious", little Irene wrote. She put her diary under her pillow and then she closed her eyes.

The next day, when she came back from school, she saw her Dad packing his bags. Maybe that was the reason they were arguing last night. *"They couldn't agree where we would go on a trip! That's right, this happens all the time!"* she thought. Irene wanted so much to believe that it was true. "Are we going on a trip?" she cheered to her Dad full of joy. "No, sweetie, Mum and I will sit down and talk to you this evening", he said with a serious look.

"He's looking at me with the eyes of work. He always has that look when he goes to the office", Irene thought and began to worry.

So, as darkness fell, holding her Teddy Bear tight in her arms, Irene dragged herself into the kitchen, where her parents were waiting for her. She noticed Mum's misty eyes but didn't say a word, she just cradled her Teddy Bear as tightly as she could.

Dad was picking at his food, swallowing it nervously and breathing heavily. *"He always acts like this when something serious happens. The last time this happened was last year, when he told me we had lost our dog"* she thought. Irene gradually realized that what was about to come out of her Dad's mouth would not be pleasant for her at all.

"Irene, we'd like to tell you something" Dad said and Irene hugged her Teddy Bear as tightly as she could. "You may have noticed that Mum and I don't agree on many things lately and that makes us yell at each other". Irene reluctantly nodded her little head. She didn't know what would be the right answer to what her Dad was telling her, so she didn't utter a word.

"As this happens all the time lately, Mum and I have decided that it would be best for all of us if we stay apart for a while" he said and Irene stared blankly. She was trying to figure out what that meant for her and her life. So many thoughts rushed through her mind at that very moment. *"Why would they stay apart? Where will Dad go? Where will I stay? Why is Mum so sad? Why does it matter if they're yelling at each other? They always make up and everything turns out just fine in the end!"* she thought, but she didn't let a single word come out of her mouth; she just let her Dad continue.

She cast her eyes over to her Mum who hadn't said a word. She looked so sad. Irene didn't have the slightest idea what to say or do. She just wanted Dad to cuddle up with Mum, like they always do in the end, so that Mum would stop being so sad. The sound of her Dad's voice interrupted her thoughts and he tried to calm her down. "Not a thing is going to change for you. We will always be your Mum and Dad and we will always love you very much; we are just going to stay apart - but you will still see both of us".

"What do you mean it's not gonna change a thing for me? It will change! You are leaving!"

In that moment she just wanted to scream. She couldn't say a word though. She felt overwhelmed by stress. She didn't understand why grown-up people always say the exact the opposite of what is actually going on. *"Since Dad is leaving, why is he telling me it's not gonna change anything for me? That's a big fat lie and they're always telling me not to tell lies"* she thought to herself. *"In…in other words?"* she muttered under her breath. "In other words, you will be spending some days here with Mum and some days at my home", he replied so naturally. "But you don't have another home?" she wondered and felt even more confused. "Well, I don't have one right now. I'm going to spend a few days at Grandma's and Grandpa's until I find my own place and then you'll be staying there too" Dad said and afterwards deep silence spread all over.

Irene's head was thumping and her stomach was growling for food – but even then she didn't utter a word. She remembered vividly all the times that Dad brought up irrelevant subjects whenever he and Mum had a serious talk which always upset Mum. The only thing she wanted was not to upset her Mum any more than she already was. So she didn't say a word. She didn't want her Mum to get even more upset.

So many unanswered questions were wandering restlessly around Irene's little head. With her tails between her legs, she dragged herself back to her room.

"But why don't my parents want to be together anymore?" she whispered into her Teddy Bear's ear as if it could understand her. "I don't know, but it's not your fault" her Teddy Bear replied... or at least that's what her little mind wanted to believe. She desperately needed to be heard by someone. "What about me? Are they going to love me like they did before? Is Dad going to leave and Mum won't be like she was before? Will Dad not play with me anymore?" she kept wondering and tears welled up in her eyes. "It's all gonna get better, don't you worry!" her Teddy Bear said. "It's all gonna get better! It's all gonna get better!" Irene repeated, trying to encourage herself.

The next day when she came back from school, Dad wasn't there. She noticed the empty bookshelves and the missing discs. Her Mum's eyes were filled with deep sorrow but Irene didn't know what to do. She went to her bedroom had to find a way to release her feelings so she grabbed her diary and began to confess…

"Monday, November 23rd 2019

My dearest diary,

The day before yesterday Dad left home. He has completely left. He packed his bags, not like going on a trip but like moving.

Days at home feel so strange without him here. Mum's always crying. Even though she's hiding in her room and doesn't let me in, so I don't see her, I know she's been crying because her eyes are constantly red when she comes out. She's never in the mood for talking or playing with me anymore. Every afternoon I speak with Dad on the phone but it doesn't feel like it did when he was at home. Every time we hang up, Mum asks me what we were talking about. I hate it when she does that, because it makes me feel really bad. I don't know what she expects me to tell her. Whatever I tell her makes her so sad. Yesterday, Dad told me that tomorrow he would come by and pick me up for a ride together. I am so happy, but I am avoiding telling Mum about it because I don't want her to feel sad . I miss my Dad a lot.

I'm so sad and my Teddy Bear is too. Oh, my Teddy Bear! How can I forget the day that Mum and Dad brought him home, so that I could hold him when I go to bed and never feel afraid of the dark again? How can I forget the moment the two of them gave me a big hug and gave me Teddy Bear as a gift? How happy was I back then, when we were all together. Now I only have my Teddy Bear to remind me those good old days. Only my Teddy Bear!", Irene wrote and then she held her Teddy tightly in her arms and asked him for help. "How I wish you could talk and tell me what to do so things would be just like they were before!", she said and tears started rolling down her cheeks.

The next day, Mum asked Irene to get ready as her Dad was on his way to pick her up.. "Will you come along, Mum?" she dared to ask. "No, sweetie, I'm going to stay here, you are going with Dad and the two of you are going to have fun" Mum replied without even looking at her. This was the first time they wouldn't all be together, and Irene began to realize how big this change was. From the moment her Mum told her that Dad was on his way, her anxiety was getting bigger and bigger. That morning she had woken up very early, in fact she could barely sleep the night before. She prepared her things; she thought of what to wear and waited anxiously for her Dad.

The doorbell rang and Irene ran to open the door filled with an overwhelming sense of longing for her Dad. As soon as she saw him, she snuggled into his arms, her heart jumping up and down with both joy and sorrow. Joy that she could see her Dad after what felt like a long time and sorrow that the three of them wouldn't be together. That feeling was so weird. She didn't know what she could do to make both her Mum and Dad happy. All she wanted was the three of them to be together but now she felt like she had to split her time between her parents and that hurt so much.

"Where would you like to go?" asked her Dad. "Wherever" said Irene. "I was thinking we could go to the playground near home so that you can see your friend Anna as well and then we can go for lunch at that fancy restaurant you like, which is next to the playground. Afterwards, we could have your favourite ice cream and in the evening, we could go to the movies if you like". Irene burst with excitement. A big "Yeah" came across her lips filled with joy and she forgot about how lonely and sad her Mum might feel.

It was a fantastic day for Irene. She played and laughed; she ate her favourite meal and watched a great movie. It was eight o'clock in the evening when Dad told her that he had to get her back home. She had mixed feelings.

She had such a great time with her Dad. It had been so long since she had felt this happy. The first thing she did when she got back home was to write everything down in her diary.

"Tuesday, November 24th 2019

My dearest diary,

Yesterday I had a really nice day with Dad. We did whatever I wanted. We played at the playground, we went to the movies, we ate ice-cream and I played with my friend Anna. It was just like we were on a school vacation and I was being spoilt with all the treats my parents would give me. Sometimes Dad spoke on the phone but most of the time he gave me his full attention. When I got back home in the evening though, Mum was really sad again. As soon as she saw me in dirty clothes, I confessed I had eaten ice cream and she got very angry with Dad. Maybe I shouldn't have told her. I hope they won't argue again because if they do, Dad may not take me out again.

Now I have to do my homework with Mum and get my ballet bag ready. I wish Dad was here and the three of us were all together like before. I wish I was doing my homework with Dad while Mum prepared dinner for us all and then put me to bed. It's weird because when I see Dad it's like I'm on vacation whereas with Mum it's like I'm at school.

A while ago I heard Mum telling Dad over the phone that she needed money for my ballet lessons and after a while she abruptly hung up on him. Why is this happening? How did my parents mess up like this?"

"Friday, November 27th 2019

 My dearest diary,

I'm feeling so sad today. Yesterday Mum told me I have to stop my ballet lessons because Dad can't afford to pay for them. She also told me that he spends all his money on his girlfriend, which I felt was strange for her to say. I couldn't figure out who that girlfriend of his was but I got really sad. How can Dad do such a thing - he knows how much I love ballet. Then Mum passed the buck to me and asked me to ask Dad for money for my ballet lessons. Just the thought of having to ask him that made me freeze.

I don't feel well - not at all - and I feel so confused. I don't want to ask Dad for money. It feels so wrong to do... but then again, if I don't do it, I will completely disappoint Mum. Today Dad came by again to take me for a walk. I didn't enjoy playing with him or having lunch. I didn't enjoy anything at all. The idea of asking him for money gripped me with fear. I don't know why. I just didn't want to do it. But I also didn't want to disappoint Mum... and so I did it.

Dad looked at me in a very strange way. Then he passed the buck back to me and told me to tell Mum to call him and the next time she wanted money, she should ask for it herself and *shouldn't put me in the middle. This situation reminded me of the game ' tug of war' that we play at school during gym class. On one side there's Dad, on the other side there's Mum, and they pull me like a rope to see which side will cross the line first.*

But I am the rope and the rope belongs to both sides. This is what they don't understand! Maybe I have to choose between them to put an end to the whole situation. I don't want to do that though; I love them both just the way they are.

I have so much fun with Dad; he makes me laugh, he spoils me with treats, helps me with my homework without yelling at me, sings to me, lets me paint and secretly buys me chocolates. On the other side, Mum is always so nice to me, even though sometimes she acts like a teacher. Every time we go out together I have such a great time, I feel like a grown-up girl. She takes me shopping, she buys me books, she comes to parties with me and my friends and she even takes me to the theatre. Oh, no, I can't lose either of them" Irene wrote and tucked the diary into her bag.

When Irene got back home, the first thing her Mum asked her about was whether she had asked her Dad about the ballet money. "Yes, I asked him!" Irene replied curtly. "What did he say to you?" her Mum asked sharply. "That the two of you gonna have a talk!" replied the little one. She was so sick and tired of being in the middle and playing Chinese whispers for both of her parents. She heard her Mum muttering through clenched teeth: "Of course, he doesn't have the guts to tell his daughter what he tells me…" or something like that but Irene couldn't quite make it out.

She wasn't in the mood to answer back to her Mum anymore. She felt so upset both by her Dad's unwillingness to give her ballet money and her Mum's rudeness towards her Dad.

"How come Dad doesn't want to pay for my ballet lessons? Maybe I should quit ballet… I'm not doing very well and I don't have many friends there… Well, maybe I don't love it as much as I thought I did the beginning and maybe it would be better if I quit…Maybe then my parents would stop arguing…How does that sound to you, Teddy Bear?"
After a while little Irene's Mum came into her room, gave her a big hug and told her that she shouldn't be upset. Eventually, Irene decided to quit ballet on her own. What mattered more to her than anything else in the world was to put an end to her parent's fighting.

"Monday, November 30th 2019

My dearest diary,

This morning someone, I don't know who, visited us and gave Mum some papers to sign. After that Mum started crying again and yelled something like: "So, he wants a divorce now! Oh, sure, he wants a new life now!" What was that all about? Why did Dad send all these papers? What's going on with him lately? Doesn't he love Mum anymore? Did quitting ballet not make a difference? Clearly not as they're arguing again. They're arguing about everything; because Dad was late to pick me up, because he didn't bring me back home on time, because he didn't pay my school tuition on time, because my clothes got dirty again, because I ate ice cream in the middle of winter and so on. It seems like I'm the thing that's causing all this trouble. What if I disappeared? Would my parents stop fighting then?" Irene wrote in her diary and started getting ready for her Dad to come and pick her up.

While she was getting ready, her Mum came into her room and told her that they would visit Grandma instead. Irene asked her Mum why their plans had changed all of a sudden and for the first time ever her Mum answered abruptly, "Because I say so and it's nothing to do with ballet. Hurry up! We're going!" Little Irene got so frustrated by her mother's bluntness that in her last-minute panic to hurry up she forgot her Teddy Bear.

"Oh, Mum, wait! I must get my Teddy Bear! Please!" said the little one, ready to burst into tears. "Irene, we need to go now!" her mother replied. "Please, it'll only take a couple of minutes!" begged Irene. "I said no, full stop!" her mother shouted and shut the door behind them. Irene couldn't help crying all the way to Grandma's. She felt painfully lonely. She had never been apart from her Teddy Bear. "Oh, come on! You're going to see Teddy Bear tonight, don't be such a baby!" her mother shouted while driving.

As soon as they arrived at Granma's, Irene quickly crawled into the bedroom. She was so furious by her mother's behaviour, that she grabbed her diary and started writing:

".. All these things happening today really got on my nerves. It was Dad's turn to come and pick me up today, but Mum brought me to Grandma's instead. She didn't even let me bring my Teddy Bear. It's the first time that Mum has yelled at me this badly. I'm sick and tired of seeing her being sad all the time…."

All of a sudden, her Grandma came in. Irene stopped writing and hid her diary under her pillow.

"What are you hiding there, sweetie?" asked Grandma even though she had got a glimpse of the diary. "I'm not hiding anything." answered Irene. "Are you sad that Mum and Dad are arguing?" Grandma asked and sat on the edge of the bed next to her. "I feel sad because I left my Teddy Bear alone back at home. Only poor Teddy Bear loves me and Mum managed to kick him out too!" yelled Irene. "Oh, I see. Aren't you sad about Mum and Dad?" Irene didn't answer back; she just shrugged her shoulders, as if she didn't want to talk about it anymore. She felt so afraid that all this was her fault.

As soon as Grandma left the room, she took out her diary again and continued writing until she drifted off to sleep.

When Grandma came back in to give her a goodnight kiss, she noticed the diary wide open and her eyes were glued to an extract from what Irene was writing:

"…I don't have the slightest clue why all this is happening to us. One thing I know for sure is that I love them both and I don't wanna see them fighting. The only dream I hold on to is to wake up one day and see them hugging one another again and me snuggling up to them the tightest I can. I can't imagine what this girlfriend of Dad is all about and why she's driven Mum completely mad. To me the only thing that matters is that Mum and Dad put an end to all this fighting. Lately I'm toying with an idea about how to help things get better, because I can't help thinking that they're fighting because of me. I'm thinking about not talking to them for a while to see if they'll stop arguing. I don't know whether my plan is going to work but there's nothing else left to do".

While Granma was totally absorbed reading all this, somewhere tucked between the diary pages, a folded napkin slipped into her hands. It was a list drawn up by the little girl. Grandma quickly took the opportunity to take a peak and started reading:

"I'll talk to you again,

-if you stop saying bad things to each other. Both of you are my parents; I love you both to the moon and back and both of are hurting ME when you are saying all these bad things to each other.

-if you stop arguing about money in front of me. I wish you shared the cost of things just like before you split up. Hearing that you don't want to pay for the things I love hurts ME.

-if you let ME play with my friends whenever I wish. It's the only time I can stay calm and not feel like my heart is broken into pieces.

-if you stop putting me in the middle and stop telling me what to say to one another. It does no good to ME. I need you to be together just like you were before. Whatever you have to argue about, do it by yourselves. I DON'T WANNA KNOW. You don't have to argue about me.

-if you stop saying that I take after the one or the other whenever I do something you don't like. I have my own personality whatever that means to you.

-if you stop talking about ME as if I were some kind of a must-have accessory. Excuses like "he couldn't come and pick her up because he was busy" isn't a nice thing to hear.

-if you decide about things that concern ME together, just like you did in the past, without fighting. I don't wanna know who supported what I wanted.

-if you follow the same rules at both houses. Different rules make ME feel confused.

-if you stop making fun of a gift that the other has given me - or telling me it wasn't that expensive. IT DOESN'T MATTER TO ME whether it was cheap or expensive; the only thing that matters to me is that you're thinking about me.

-if you stop arguing about whom I will spend the holidays or my birthday with. What would definitely be ideal for ME is to spend holidays and my birthday with both of you!

And I want you to know that I don't have any problem meeting other people that happen to be in your life, but I'm not sure whether I'm going to like them or not… but they can be part of my family too, as long as they love me!

Irene, your Daughter"

Grandma read every word and understood everything. She didn't say a word about it to Irene's Mum though. A couple of days later Irene put her secret plan into action. She had been so sick and tired of all these quarrels taking place all the time that she didn't want to hear any more. Every time they argued, she would cover her ears and start singing to her Teddy Bear as loud as she could. One day, she made the big decision to implement her plan. After considering it all over again and again, she made up her mind that this would be the best thing to do. The time had come. She decided not to speak to either of them and kept her promise.

That evening when she arrived home, Irene didn't say a word to her Mum, as much as she tried to tease out something of her. "Did you have a good time with Grandma?", "Are you upset that you didn't see your Dad?", "Don't worry, you won't lose your Dad…", "Do you realize that your Dad will leave home and move on with his life?", "Aren't you gonna eat something?" she kept asking again and again. Days were passing by and Irene's Mum kept bombarding her with all these questions. They remained unanswered though.

She did the same thing with her Dad too. When he came to pick her up she didn't run to hug him and she didn't act glad to see him. She was very angry with both of them.

All the attempts her Dad made in order to apologize fell in vain. "Sorry I didn't come the other day but your Mum took you to Grandma's and wouldn't let me come to pick you up", "Are you upset because of those papers?", "Are you sad that we're gonna be apart?" "It's the best thing for all of us, so we stop arguing!", "Would you mind if I introduced you to a friend of mine that I have been hanging out with?" Don't worry; I'm not gonna let Mum take you away from me" "How about we go for an ice cream together?". Days were passing by and Dad also kept asking Irene more and more questions but she maintained her stony silence.

For the next ten days Irene was so determined to stick to her plan, she kept her stubborn silence and didn't speak to anyone, not just her parents, but also anyone at school, or anywhere else. She noticed though that her parents quit all their arguing. When they spoke on the phone, her Mum whispered to her Dad, so that Irene couldn't hear. They both seemed to be really worried about her.

One day Grandma came by and she and Mum were talking for hours in the kitchen. Then Grandma came into Irene's room. "Sweetie, it's Grandma! Don't you even want to talk to me?" There was no answer back and silence conquered the room. "Hey, listen, sweetie! I know all about your secret plan! I know that you quit talking to your parents just because they're arguing all the time. I also know about that list of yours!" Grandma whispered to her granddaughter. Even then, Irene didn't reply, although she looked at her full of curiosity as if she wanted to ask her how on earth she knew all that.

Nevertheless, the little one maintained her silence. After a couple of hours, she ran towards her Grandma and put the napkin with the list into her hands. "Please, Grandma, help me be heard! That's all I want!" she said and fell into her comforting arms. Of course, poor Teddy Bear couldn't be left out of this so much needed big warm hug. He was her supporting pillar after all. Grandma held the napkin with the list tightly in her hands and tears were rolling slowly down her cheeks. She went back to the kitchen where her daughter was waiting, grabbed her hand, put the napkin into her palm and said: "Read it carefully and always remember this with every decision you make in your life. And give this napkin to Irene's Dad too!"

Eventually this is how little Irene made her voice heard, stronger and clearer than ever. Her parents' once boosted egos began to fall apart.

A new relationship was built between them and both now knew they had to make up a new communication and friendship code, even if they weren't living together anymore. Now pure love and waves of tenderness were sweeping over their most magnificent creation, their own child.

"Don't worry that children never listen to you; *worry* *that they are* *always watching you."*

ROBERT FULGHUM

"The sign of great parenting *is not* *the children's behavior.*

The sign of great parenting *is the parent's behavior."*

ANDY SMITHSON

Please submit a review on Amazon for this book. I would love to hear your feedback.

Printed in Great Britain
by Amazon